Inside My World

MEET MY PET

By Tina Benajmin

Gareth Stevens
PUBLISHING

Please visit our website, www.garethstevens.com. For a free color catalog of all our high-quality books, call toll free 1-800-542-2595 or fax 1-877-542-2596.

Library of Congress Cataloging-in-Publication Data

Benjamin, Tina, author.
Meet my pet / Tina Benjamin.
pages cm. — (Inside my world)
Includes index.
ISBN 978-1-4824-1798-2 (pbk.)
ISBN 978-1-4824-1796-8 (6 pack)
ISBN 978-1-4824-1797-5 (library binding)
1. Pets—Juvenile literature. I. Title.
SF416.2.B46 2015
636—dc23

2014027570

First Edition

Published in 2015 by
Gareth Stevens Publishing
111 East 14th Street, Suite 349
New York, NY 10003

Editor: Ryan Nagelhout
Designer: Sarah Liddell

Photo credits: Cover, p. 1 (background) Evgeny Atamanenko/Shutterstock.com; cover, p. 1 (pets) Eric Isselee/Shutterstock.com; pp. 5, 7, 9, 11, 13, 24 (feathers) Alena Ozerova/Shutterstock.com; pp. 15, 17, 19, 21, 23 sonya etchison/Shutterstock.com; p. 24 (seeds) Lara Uster/Shutterstock.com.

Printed in the United States of America

CPSIA compliance information: Batch #CW15GS: For further information contact Gareth Stevens, New York, New York at 1-800-542-2595.

Contents

I love my pet.

I have a parrot.
Her name is Lucy.

I give Lucy a kiss.
She has blue feathers
on her wings.

Lucy can talk!
She repeats what I say.

I feed her
out of my hand.
She likes seeds.

My friend Jordan
has a pet, too.

Jordan has a dog.
His name is Lucky.

Lucky is
a golden retriever.

Jordan likes
to hug Lucky.

His brother helps him give Lucky a bath.

Words to Know

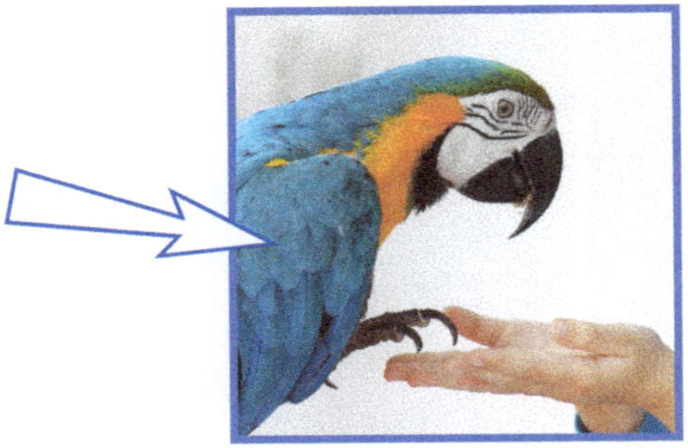

feathers

seeds

Index